A Fun Rhyming Picture Book About Family, Travel, and Discovering Kentucky

I SPY KENTUCKY

**Written by
Ladie Warfield**

**Illustrated By
The BM Group**

isbn 13: 979-8-9995689-2-2

The first stop is school. Mia admires the murals on the wall; Muhammad Ali, horse races, and diversity. There's something there for us all.

It's Hot Brown Day in the lunchroom line,
But Mom says, "Hurry up! We have to leave on time!"

The city grows smaller, the sky opens wide.
The road feels like magic as we ride.

We stop at a diner for warm cherry pie. "It's so good!" Mia smiles at the cashier. "I'd eat the whole pie if I could."

As we walk back to the car,
"Hey, y'all!" a stranger calls out with cheer.
That friendly Kentucky hello rings loud and clear.

We take a break at a small-town park where the oak trees grow. Mama and I play basketball. "Bounce! Bounce! Throw

The road twists higher through colors that gleam.
The hills look like a quilt stitched red, gold, and green.

Church bells chime where the coal tipples stand.
Old, rusty beams whisper of hard work in the land.

We pass the vibrant, hand-painted signs with a big grin.
"Bluegrass Festival!" we read again and again.

The porch swing creaks with a welcoming sound. Grandma wraps me in her arms, lifting my feet off the ground.

Inside her kitchen, the smell is so sweet.
Soup beans and cornbread, my favorite treat.

She tells of the river, the hills, and the mysteries of the mine. Her voice makes even the scariest of stories shimmer and shine.

www.ingramcontent.com/pod-product-compliance
Lightning Source LLC
Chambersburg PA
CBRC090842120626
46551CB00008B/731